# MAKERSPACE PLAY

## MAKE & PLAY

# HARDWARE STORE

Rebecca Felix

Consulting Editor, Diane Craig,
M.A./Reading Specialist

**Super Sandcastle**

An Imprint of Abdo Publishing
abdobooks.com

# abdobooks.com

Printed in the United States of America, North Mankato, Minnesota
052021
092021

THIS BOOK CONTAINS
RECYCLED MATERIALS

Design: Sarah DeYoung, Mighty Media, Inc.
Production: Mighty Media, Inc.
Editor: Liz Salzmann
Cover Photographs: Mighty Media, Inc.; Shutterstock Images
Interior Photographs: iStockphoto; Mighty Media, Inc.; Shutterstock Images

The following manufacturers/names appearing in this book are trademarks: Duck Tape®

Library of Congress Control Number: 2020949943

**Publisher's Cataloging-in-Publication Data**
Names: Felix, Rebecca, author.
Title: Make & play hardware store / by Rebecca Felix.
Description: Minneapolis, Minnesota : Abdo Publishing, 2022 | Series: Makerspace play
Identifiers: ISBN 9781532195877 (lib. bdg.) | ISBN 9781098216603 (ebook)
Subjects: LCSH: Play--Juvenile literature. | Hardware stores--Juvenile literature. | Toys-- Juvenile literature. | Creative ability in children--Juvenile literature. | Imagination in children--Juvenile literature.
Classification: DDC 790.1922--dc23

Super SandCastle™ books are created by a team of professional educators, reading specialists, and content developers around five essential components—phonemic awareness, phonics, vocabulary, text comprehension, and fluency—to assist young readers as they develop reading skills and strategies and increase their general knowledge. All books are written, reviewed, and leveled for guided reading and early reading intervention programs for use in shared, guided, and independent reading and writing activities to support a balanced approach to literacy instruction.

## TO ADULT HELPERS

The projects in this book are fun and simple. There are just a few things to remember to keep kids safe. Some projects may use sharp or hot objects. Also, kids may be using messy supplies. Make sure they protect their clothes and work surfaces. Be ready to offer guidance during brainstorming and assist when necessary.

# CONTENTS

# MAKE & PLAY

Do you ever wonder what it would be like to run a store or other business? Why not try it and find out? You can turn your makerspace into a pet supply store or grocery store or even an **arcade**! This book will show you how to make your very own hardware store.

# MAKE & PLAY STEPS

Step 1 GET INSPIRED ☑

Step 2 BRAINSTORM ☑

Step 3 GET READY ☑

Step 4 MAKE! ☑

Step 5 PLAY! ☑

## Makerspace Rules

1. **Ask.** Ask an adult if it's okay to make your hardware store. Ask for help when using sharp or hot tools. These include craft knives and glue guns.

2. **Keep Trying.** Don't give up when things don't work as planned. Instead, think about the problem you are having. What are some ways to solve it?

3. **Be Nice.** Share space and supplies with other makers.

4. **Clean Up.** Put things away when you are finished working. Find a safe space to store unfinished projects until next time.

# IMAGINE A HARDWARE STORE

You've probably gone to a hardware store many times. But have you ever thought about how amazing this type of store is?

Hardware stores sell many kinds of tools and supplies. You can get nails, screws, hammers, paint and paintbrushes, and more! Hardware stores also sell products for gardens and homes. These include seeds, plants, and gloves. What are your favorite parts of a hardware store?

THINK ABOUT THE HARDWARE STORES YOU'VE BEEN TO. WHAT DID YOU SEE THERE? YOU MIGHT EVEN TAKE A TRIP TO A HARDWARE STORE TO GET IDEAS!

# BRAINSTORM

Now it's time to think about your own hardware store. What products will you sell? What services will you provide? Try to think through all the details, from special displays to uniforms.

I want a paint sample station that helps people pick out paint colors.

9

# GET READY

Now it's time to gather what you need to create your store. Cardboard could be used to create tools. Maybe you need card stock for paint **samples**.

Turn cardboard and aluminum foil into tools for sale.

Use connectors such as rubber bands and duct tape.

Create gardening products out of recycled bottles, **containers**, and bowls.

Think of other supplies you could use. How about craft foam, chenille stems, paint, toothpicks, or wire?

Ask an adult before you use any furniture, sharp tools, or other supplies for your store!

# MAKE!

It's time to create your hardware store! Work with others to make different parts of the store. Help one another solve problems along the way.

Tape wooden and cork objects together to make a hammer. Cover the head with foil.

**Will your store sell tools?**
Then you'll need to make the tools and a display to hold them!

Stick craft foam circles to the ends of toothpicks to make nails.

Wrap wire around golf tees to make screws.

Make a pegboard out of a piece of cardboard. Poke evenly spaced holes with a skewer.

13

**Will your store have employees?**

Then you'll need to make uniforms!

Cut up an old T-shirt to make an employee's vest.

Cut a rectangle out of leather to make a tool belt. Weave strips through each end. Make sure they are long enough to tie around the waist.

Cut out leather shapes to make pockets. Glue the bottom and sides of each shape to the tool belt.

HANNAH'S Hardware

Decorate a pin-back button with paper, glue, and markers to make a store logo tag.

**Will your hardware store sell paint?**

Then you'll need to create paint **samples** and painting tools for customers.

Rosebud 2343
Watermelon 2345
Cherry Red 2347
Coral Sand 6895
Island Sunrise 6893
Island Sunset 6891

Sunshine 1295
Rubber Ducky 1291
Pear 7104
Key Lime 7106
Frog 7108

9504
Caribbean 9502
Aqua 9500
Sky 5850
Baby Blue 5848
Cookie Monster 5846

Lavender 8826
Lilac 8824
Grape 8822
Cotton Candy 3954
Bubblegum 3952
Barbie 3950

Turn empty jars into paint **sample containers**. Label them to match the sample cards.

Make a paint roller. Glue large bottle caps to the ends of a cardboard tube. Have an adult help you make a hole in one of them first. Wrap a piece of pool noodle around the tube. Stick a **bundle** of skewers through the hole.

Make a handle out of paint stir sticks. Tape the handle to the bundle of skewers.

Cut rectangles out of card stock for paint sample cards. Paint each one a different color. Add color names and product numbers too!

Lavender
8826

Lilac
8824

Grape
8822

Co+

Aqua
9500

Cherry

Grape

LIVING IN WAYZATA

17

**Will your hardware store have a garden section?**

Make gardening goods to sell. These can include seeds, gloves, a watering can, and more!

BEET

CARROT

BEANS

Use disposable silverware and plates to make gardening tools such as trowels and rakes.

Have an adult help you cut up plastic bottles and **containers**. Duct tape them together to make a watering can.

Create seed packets out of paper. Use tiny beads for the seeds.

Add patterns of puff paint to cotton gloves to make gardening gloves.

TOMATO

# PLAY!

It's time to bring all your creations together to make your hardware store complete. Add any final **details** and finishing touches. Then invite friends, family, teachers, or classmates to come shop at your store!

# HARDWARE STORES & MORE

How did your hardware store turn out? Did you think of other elements you could add to the store? Keep inviting new people to play and **brainstorm**. You never know what fun ideas they might have!

When you're finished playing with your hardware store, remember to clean up. Put things back where you found them. Then think about your next makerspace project! What other stores or businesses would you like to make and play?

# GLOSSARY

**arcade** – a place with many games that can be played by putting coins in them.

**brainstorm** – to come up with a solution by having all members of a group share ideas.

**bundle** – a group of things tied together.

**container** – something that other things can be put into.

**detail** – a small part of something.

**disposable** – made to be used once and then thrown away.

**sample** – a small amount of something that is given to people to try.

**trowel** – a small gardening tool with a curved blade used for digging and planting.